One Solitary Journey
Into
The Inner Rivers

Written by:
Rachel Dillemuth

Edited and Revised by:
Kainalu Wilson

Inactivity is the lowest point of the wave...
the easiest ride.
                ... the crest is colder in the waters...yet...
it is also the peaking. . . the thrusting out . . .
        and too, risking the dashing on the rocks.

        I may avoid being dashed upon the rocks at
the expense of never basking upon the warm sands
                        of peace. . . .

The Introduction....

One tiny drop of rain mingles with the downpour – one downpour mingles with the rivers, on to the seas, and back to the stars. Each in life separate – while mixing together at different levels to form newer life. As with humans, they too, have drops of water in the inner caverns of the soul.

To follow the waters may lead to the tapping of the internal rivers. When one dips into the sources of the inner creativity a brief awareness state opens onto new thresholds of aliveness. This diminishes none of being alive as previously felt, rather, for a moment, rises the tide level to greater feelings of the knowledge of 'life'.

When the rivers are open and the flow of the energy is tapped for external display in the forms of all arts or mental thinking, one can not recede the waters; they come not as called upon – coming instead, as they already exist.

My rivers have always existed, running strong,
totally illusive, beyond grasp, to be felt more
then lived. In these offerings the changing
relationships within and without have jellied the
Illusive thoughts into a mass that is actual.

It is.....For one.....The land rising from the marshes.

The marshes have always been alive with all
forms of matter and all of the elements, in primal
forms, in a stagnate media. When new fertility washes
deep in the currents of the marsh it is the basis
for 'new' land to rise and new land is the foundation
for greater being and fresher foundings for the
totality of existence. This is the 'Aliveness' of
the reflections....

A child is a life form and only one life
form. It is not the whole of the self, nor the
basis of life for the mother, nor the motivation
for life in itself. It is a mirror ... ostensibly a
showing of the fertile soil which was planted.

Most seeds will flourish in adequate conditions.
The past condition shave always had adequate substance
upon which to survive. The idea of being more
'Alive' is merely a bubbling of the rivers tapped
to the surface...

A different plane...

Not a new or a find in the thoughts of
existence, rather a find of one individual into
the self.

I am afraid, yet ... fear is also only one
Level. It has stifled the emergence of the inner
seedlings and bent the heads of unfelt passions.
Passions of the soul can dwell as external arms to
stimulate one's environment into a feeling media
or they can remain hidden in the stagnations of
the marshes.

It is a gift – access to the rivers ...
It is not a gift to be donned with ornations ...
rather ... one glimpse into the inner travesty of the
side roads concealed in each being – a seed in
cystic form thirsting for the waters that signal
its germination. Peaks of highs retract themselves
estranged from those highs which are real in the
obtaining of deeper levels of the spiritual – If
there is one who can distinguish those spiritual
values from those every day consequences, then
there is one who knows the inner rivers deeper
than i...

     This is the growth – deception of words
hollow in their follies of understanding and
conveyance of meaning. You too are tapping your
inner rivers and may in the reflections of yourself
be experiencing the land rising from the marshes.

     Each level has a different tune to be sung by
its conceiver yet the harmonics are one in the
universe.

     Intellectual comprehension of the states
of existence has no cosmic validity except
in one's own reality sphere and the words matter
little except to pass the time of existence.

     With this, peace and happy understanding...
                    The author.

Now with more thought to the aspects of the rivers ...

... The final Don Juan experience would be to draw from the sources as desired — maintaining that 'man' in the course of life is not so much the destiner of the self as he is the

Destinee with all.

"Now I Understand poems entitled 'Fragments'"

My mind crushed beneath the
        weight of thoughts lying bared (waiting)
to nurse the fledglings from their daze.

No legs to pace them on,
        no tongue to sound the beating of their wings-
Hands hang mute.

Surges-retreats. . .anchoring tight
        in the crevices of the naval,
Awaiting the shedding of self encagement.

Thoughts powerfully rein the
        Muscles that move them onward-
soaring from the tensioned body.

Peace, drench birth of that space into
        whose globals they enter in
flight above the cortex.

The Beginnings. . . . .

There was a time when an inner force existed that was separate from the dichotomy of the intel-Lectual and the feeling selves. It never left, so to speak, as much as the outer ego self became heavily involved in a defining of the selves by pattern segmentation of their interaction with Surrounding energies. Those energies relate to 'survival-maintaining' in a noisy, clashing environment which seemed a cesspool of wasted motion of objects, people, and their ego status'.

Now out of the inner center of my being comes not the void - surrounded by the conflict of the emotional self and coated by the intellectual thinking self - now where existed void is the Reviving of the cosmic. . . very warm fluid swirling motions . . .oozing through and beyond the physical self. An integrating yet detaching space as those things which held roles of importance in my being are sent out (concerns) and away where dealing with them is still necessary, but only a function and not the driving tendrillar force, gripping and splintering the interior as before. . .

The plotting out of one's pace with time is ceasing as a flowing level emerges. In life's conflicts there is some variation — the changing of one trauma into a new one. . .Yet the eminence of those 'traumas' are lost and non-existent. Their place has been diminished to a finer point on the ever diluting plane of an over all existence state.

There has been an actualisation process in motion — less splitting of the thinking and feeling selves as they find a common ground in the fluid inner energy.

I am being born — not a separate individual who has a demanding ego self . . . Born rather as a Small part of a universal flowing through which all beings exist and find ground for the essence of all matter.

. . . . Hypokimenon.

"One man's life is but a shooting star across a galaxy of time - separate - yet part of a totality - pure energy converging into matter back to energy" – self quote by Author

Civilisation has cultivated complex structures
to plot out an order of those thing surrounding
mankind. What was once a tool to the survival in
its base form in animal history has become compulsive
behavior in the guise of expedient technology. It is now
insistent upon laying a format upon which each element -
whether it stem of nature or of human creation - can be
dissected, labeled, and repackaged in a way it becomes
comprehensible to the eyes of the human brain.

Nature is more subtle and is less discerning
About founding separate entities in her being. There
is within her a unity lacking in man's shell being.
It is in this shell form that for mankind Life equates
Death, in living form, and Death = Life.
Death, in itself, is a threat to mankind. . . something to be
poked and prodded until it recedes along with the fear of loss
of the ego self into the inner folds of the mind. It is an
obstacle - an ending
accepted not as a cycle among other cycles but an
abyss in the mountains.

A single tree can exist not of itself. . .for
in doing so which parts then constitute a tree or
a plant (Or a man?)? Is it the trunk. . .the
outreaching branches, green with growth or yellow
as death approaches. . .

Or. . .is a tree the dead leaves scattered around
or the bands of black mulch of leaf and branch
fragments. . . are they not also part of a 'tree'?
Maybe a tree is the root system stretching out
creating the major portion of a 'tree' yet are
viewed not by an observer of that 'tree'.

Trees and plants are all of those things, the
soil, the new growth, the seed from which they
germinate. . .

The continuing cycles of the natural environment
leave little to be established as a split energy. . .

Each and every particle shares not the other, and yet is
one with all. . .

In the beginning to my first seed. . .

. . .the only thing I want to say which does
not help your survival of yourself for yourself
- - I love you.

. . .there can be no taking back of the hard
times I've given you. . . I can love you today and
tomorrow will handle itself as there are no mistaken
disbursements of energy in its flow so accept
my love, reject my guilt and be open to
everything. . .

THE STIRRINGS. . . .

Where are those words
        Caressing my silent tongue?
They are gone/playing hide and seek
        with my pen and paper.

Uncover yourselves!
        Stop this foolish game. . .
It is not the 'me' who
        bears truth with wisdom. . . .

It could be the words - a feeling
        existence mused into outer voids-
A feeling sent out - maybe
        You too touch it.

Another truth is simple -
        the poem is only a symbol
        Of our weakest media -
        Words.

Reaction. . . . . .

Once,

        I sat. . .and wrote some words -

Then,

        I sat. . .and felt those words -

And behold -
        There lay before me -
                a poem.

THE STRUGGLES......

My spirit doesn't want to die. . . but to live stretching out of the shell of my body. I mentally feel that enclosure of the inner self and desire to know how to freely flow amidst my inner self. Neither has the knowledge of the self borne fruit in the passions of living.

It is all Maya - all knowing/
Knowing not at all.

If there is any validity to the 'knowledge' of life stemming within, then where are the seeds of mental growth? There resembles nothing of the core signifying peace or the end of strife.   It is as if the feeling self is all strife.
I damn the world because I've been damned. . .I seek contentness because all has been war. . .Yet I live war as what I know. . . it comes. . .boiling over at a moments notice - - - unaware of it insidious venom creeping through the brain. . . spewing out its vengeance.

. . .I know naught of love but seek to live it.
Can it be part of the existence without prior
absorption?   Will my concepts of fulfillment
remain in Maya or will the dawn of peace come
when cessation of desire passes- - -allowing
illusion to be what is actual?

Is the desire of contentment only Maya in
itself?

Nevertheless it is a fools hell. . .taunting
fingers of an inner incompetence that pursue the
voices drifting in their cellular void.
A brain never soaking its circuits in peace. . .
God be damned! . . .the ground of being scorched in
hell. Neitche suggests that hell is the Dionysus
of living purpose or is the hell the fruit of
over fulfillment?

I was going to write of revolution.
Here on the dunes, city lost, ocean soaring from
the curve of our spherical platter. . . revolution
transits to freedom.

Freedom from/as revolution against- - -archaic
forms man has destined to their graves. We have
far developed the seats of our grave from our
own attempts to escape from- - -each other, oppression,
hunger, death,
conquest from/against. . .

Those who seek freedom seek reversal. . .
freedom to/revolution toward. . . Neither to be gained
in our realms of nepotism. That which the sixties
deemed as establishment and those they condemned as
oppressive pigs - that too will destine itself to
a suicidal subsmission.
. . .Burial forms from their own plateaus of
success.

For the young 'revolutionist' where are your
goals? . . .Belie they in counter destruction and
verbal abuse too?

There is more to the games than selecting
the right boxes. . .
They must be balanced; complementing
each other's existence without being structurally
dependent in the whole of the foundation.
A blueprint to the balance is useless.
The touch is yours. . . mine. . .the flow. . .through which
the right 'be-ings' assemble and reassemble similar
to the bonding and unbonding of atoms and electron
associates in molecular chains as introduce to
variants of matter. . .They will balance themselves.

To be. . .more in planarian levels is to allow
others to be. . . especially a child. . .
Allow them to be. . . as they are
(no idealism intended at this point)

In a day to day jaunt I seem to stumble among
the rocks and forget they, too, are only illusion
and will stand until the flow whittles them down into
the bits of soil they once were.
   Their presence stand as do the products of our
embodiments . . .standing like false gods before us.

   False gods. . . blinding to the inner eye - false
gods - the whole of civilization deplores them.
Idealistically their only 'Gods' lie in the Hope-
the goodness - the religion.

   Alas; The actual gods have not the
question of morality of the religious Ideal God.
These very real 'Gods' are the commodities, the
gifts of 'real' things to appease our shells. . .

   There is not time to get if we lose ourselves
in the mires of 'pathos', 'eros', or 'charity'. The
giving is thought more to be done somewhere to the
Self.
   If we give it seems a loss unmeasured by the
ideal 'values', rather, it is weighted in sacrifices
to our false gods.

The struggle continues. . .
	in reflections on and to the second seed bearer. .

My dear sir. . . here's to the day of the verdict. . .
	. . .whatever it will be the times will move on
and the tides are continuous but melancholy stays
pendant over my pool.

	Those days of subdued fear are passing. I
can go on and try to remember in its incorporation
the gentleness of spirit, the easy flow. . .I can be
with or without. . .though there are days the horizon
blackens and the thought of separation over the
contradictions of justice weigh heavy upon me.

You have spoken of rats fleeing a sinking ship. . .

       Oh, you are not sinking. . .nothing of
you has changed - only the circumstances of your
Flow. . .Only the shadows cast on the lawn have
shifted . . . . .

          . . . . .the trees are standing as before.

THE TRANSISTING......

A person can die spiritually and be physically Alive. Or a person can die his ego death giving way to the cosmic alive/ness.

Most people are living 'dead'. For some, they have glimpsed cosmic alive/ness only to retreat to the living death because the letting go (which is simple in its base nature and intellectual concept) is too difficult to live out as living alive.

By not doing and just being (a fine balance) can one satori and maintain levels of higher consciousness.

Which. . . into leads, progressively,
The Act.
. . . the focusing of an inner awareness towards the world.

Looking backwards is usually not in the direction
of integration. . . .

Sleep's state of dreams has softened and
somewhere the interior must have seeded itself. . .
             Trance dreams have flown above the conscious
                      - -not quite centering inwardly.
        I rise. . .conscious, still, of my body - distant
though paralleling the distance is the visual
image of a rising peak. . .

The completeness of the act. . .

There can be borders - confines - to the cosmic awareness (It is a matter of the doors you choose to open isnt it) . . .yet it can not be tucked away in the clouds of an acid's fantasy or an inner trance state.

We are neither ego shell nor cosmic – for one (for the individual) can not exist estranged from the other.

No man is an island, <u>true.</u> and at the same time is exactly that.   Cosmically he/she is all Matter - no shell. Ego wise, the individual, is very much the island.

People can not enter another's conscious and eliminate nor share the inner pain, the love, the feeling ego that is measurable only within the self and, correspondingly, resolution can come only from the same self and not someone else's reality.

Our shells remain fixtures limited in their modes of release. . .the cosmos is limitless and all the energy of the spheres goes with us.

Awareness. . . the awakening . . . . . dare I enter?

Our total perception and all intellectual
processes go through our own channels. . . each
deviated through patterns developed to help the
survival of our psychic and its shell and out
emotional components, which is for each Ego reality
a substantial part/our primitive part.

Delegation of The Pairs as those things good
and those things bad, will not lead to the flow.
Life is neither good or bad. . . it is . . .

that is the sum and the figures total
a perfect circle. . . absolute nil . . . the zero/ing of
all matter back unto. . .

Itself . . . Yourself.

It is much to the unknowing - and potentially destroying knowledge - to the living 'dead' - the en masses who thread their goodness of humanity on the hope of the nirvana - the heaven of promised rewards from an unjust world - Much to these is the lacking awareness of the impotence of their God. . . .

The christ. . . the intangible source whose very intangibility, in form, is designated for him by the 'christians' of the world.

Their savior is invalid.
He is of the <u>outer</u> - - which - - cosmically, is non-existent.

Teach not his impotence, for in doing so you equivocally unbraid the shred of psychic (held by estimations to be 70% of the general populace) left to be their glue.

Theirs is the assurance that some other worldly power is responsible for their salvation, damnation, and deliverance -

other - than <u>themselves</u>!

The world started its creation in the spirit
of its Godhood. . . that's what the bible says. . .only
it seems to have omitted the the Godhood is within
the external organism from which we have life. . .the
Eden is within. . . wait, wait . . . So-hung
So-hung
So-hung. . .

The sound of the Godhood-
the breather of the universe-
So-hung -
So-hung . . .

It is also the sound of your own breath.

Carl jung was a man called the Father of
something or another in the science of Psychology.
More still, he was a man who did not ask the world
to offer validity to his thought he simply said,
So to speak -
        Here is my thought - - to prove or to
disprove is of little interest to me - that is
your game. . .

        Myself, I am still caught in the 'seeing'
and the 'doing'.

THE MIRRORING BEFORE THE POOL. . . .

You may lapse yourself into the pragmatics
of keeping the details of your life together and
forget the happiness . . . .the attitude . . . the movement
so circumvented by language in the totally inadequate
word . . . the flow . . .

If we continually thread our needle - the
eye of ourselves - with the thread of the future
then we would never arrive at any moment of peace
or contentedness.   Nor can we patch our current
positions with the remnants of our past wether
it is the good or the bad. If, as it were, we
lose the thread to our present under the details
of things that have to be done, the things will
 get done at the expense of our inner selves.
        This is just thinking how it is when the
externals become so demanding and taxing upon us
we forget to relax the brow and be happy or that
in the midst of it all that we CAN be happy.

Every writer, regardless of the symbology,
is seeking and/or expostulating the 'I' . To be
honest in the pursuit of the art of scribbling is
to get to the point - - the immediacy of the 'It/I'.
  If in writing, we bury the I in words and
abstracts we have succeeded in boxing more of our
world. . . wrapping it up neatly, securing a place
for a partial yet defined self.

  The totality of all things written and spoken
in the annals of science and every facet of
civilization does not answer the basic individual
quest for the 'Who of the I'.
  You might think we should look and see the
blatant insignificance of our acquested dynasties. . .
yet, we still search.

  Because of the search we can not be. . . we can
be only when we stop looking - for the self is
already in the time from the moment the spore rooted
in the silt.
  We exist. . .
    I exist.

The reflections of the levels. . . of consciousness -
　　shell existence - and of self development.
　　My core level is a very cool experience;
It is the spirit of the mountains. . .fullness.
　　Most difficult is the sub-level between my
outer casing and the core. Between core and the
sub-level is the horizontal line - the space -
a bit of the galaxies where the self is quite void
and usually immobile when that nullification of
the material source occurs.
　　The sub-L. Is, imaginably, a level in people,
the one in which rests all of the neurosis' , psychosis'
and mental disorders - - the breeder of the hatred,
the guilt, and the bondage of self sufferance. . .

　　Beware, for it can be so inflammatory that it,
if not untwisted, will gnarl the deeper woods.

The time has come to open a clear expression
for the self, not for the world (leave the world
out of private welfare) and to move gently in spirit
and to check the fires of the undercoating - lighting
as it does in tremendous waves so unexplainable,
so isolating, and so stagnating.

(No one should need cigarettes and valium to
Do that. . .) It is such an immeasurable solution
and when the catalystic forces have ceased and
solidification is measurable then, then in this
time lies no desire, need, or purpose in trying
to measure. When the self is centered and sends
forth the embodiment into the world the cringe
is gone as the force pushes out, closing the paths
for the outer arrows to congregate and needle the
self levels.

Time and work, for expectations seem to hold
up empty hands and embittered souls - while the
work of the centered fills the gaps and dispels
into the timeless spheres.

This (can be)
the reversing of the currents so instead of fighting
to go across the stream or up it I move in time with it.

When a segment of your mind that acts as the inner eye becomes bored with the <u>Real</u> things in life, try to get in touch with the fantasy side (Not that there is any difference). . .

I fantasize of late of Paris - - the city of class vulgarity done on a plateau of finesse, having drawn to its chest most of history's fervent philosophers, writers, and artisans so each gifted in the crafts of their souls. . .a city in which I may never set forth. . .yet . . .

You see — for some there never need exist the reality of the fantasy only the freedom to exist in the fantasy and. . . the continued freedom to always recognize the pitfalls of illusion (enchantment - the suave of the mind). . . And. . .

Finally, in that recognition (recognition of the fantasy's cosmic invalidity), in that, belies the ultimate freedom to transist to be/ing. . .

(in regards to that fantasy)

Logically, that process applies to love.

    If, for one, the task of love (caring about, etc.)- If for one it is a threat or when love goes its way there is a loss beyond the departure, then there is also no being or flow.

    When, for one, Love can be interexchanged and then parted and there suffers no loss of the ego/comic then only can love come forth freely.

    There are no confines - -no depletion - -
no <u>CONSUMPTION!</u>

    It is within (theoretically) of the Dissolution of Pairs - - that loss/gain - - that feelings can take wing and be flowered.

    Not much to say but a hell of a thing to do.

Have we forgotten our womb?
    Lay we softly in fluid space - born ever
so gently in our wraps of silence.
We came from that womb into the spaces
    Not so fluid and wrapped not of itself.
under the juices of the sensual.

We have come to the non/state from one of the cosmic.
    It crowds our senses with hardness and
the adaptation often despairs its way into us -
    then the hardness becomes ours.

What (in soft remembrance) do we offer our own?
    Theirs too, was the tactile - the elludement of mass. And
theirs was the celestial in the platonist hyperbola.
We caress the child not with the salts of the palms
    Nor with the embraces of unchecked nurturing -
Rather all space seems splintered with verbal strokes

Could it be that we are afraid?
    Speech lessens only 'our' pain of silence
Dare we in our unfolding touch through the air. . .
    out . . .with our energy?

It is in our human condition that. . .

a crying child can hear the
    soothing banters of our verbal offerings.

it is in our human condition that. . .

A crying child can absorb the warmth
    of bodies pressed with theirs.

it is in our social condition that. . .

To raise and to teach we strive
    as a 'mother' to a 'child'.

it is in our universal condition that. . .

To love and to comfort we flow
    as people with children.

it is in our infinite condition that. . .
To be aware of only one moment,
        and of no other - we transcend as one. . .
                with ALL.

Second thoughts in the mirroring before the pool. . .

How much are we conditioned to view blue-collar work,
non-productive types, and the less polished as lesser parts
around us? Only college is good, only the waves of tokenism of
the work ethic - - paper sheaths of knowledge - -paper words
of dimensions of what we are – that – and numbers.

What greater the task is to be productive
only within and around the self. To do of the
self - - not to be confused with the functions of
the shell self (which is often just the mirrored
face of other's states of lacking).
When one completes it seldom is with an ease. . .
It usually pairs the consuming form of completion.
As ... a parent completes in part a child's world –
as they fill the times of boredom, the needs of
touch, and the filling of an empty stomach. . .
Just as toys fill the mind's imagery to create
Play. . . and people fill the gaps of nothing to do
        . . .sometimes they hinder.

The POOLING. . . . .

Psychedelic dreams - shell trip nightmares –
the mind boils and the spirit thrashes about in
confused dionysian webs – no rains come to cool
the city's scorched streets. Echos bounce in the
inner corridors and a bed lies empty.

The cup tilts and spills the dye streaking
the empty hallways with the blood of the gods. . .All
color, all grayness, all sound bound in stifled
undertones of nothing.

So sits the soul - - castle walls crumble and
corridors in their disergregation* overflow and ooze
space, salting the pores in the outer ducts.

No longer cobweb thoughts clinging to gray
walls and hollow floors – now blown free by the
space in the crumbled stone edifices they spin
forward in a mist – a fleck in the eye of the
universe.

So sits my soul in its fallen castle and opened
mazes. . Boxed emptiness moves to open galaxies.

(tracing, 'tis the len's illusion).

So soars my soul and the dreams and the
nightmares merge 'till the mass is dissolved in
it's own hardness and. . .

So sit I in numbness.

*Disergregation. . .

The breaking down of the universal workforce.

It goes on forever. . .the thoughts rambling through the mind. . .

Formation of the ideas is easy. . .the dispersing of the same is more difficult. Like the sea, the mind's activities are never ceasing. 'Breaks' in the ever flowing elements such as time are to be created more in the mind then in life's daily Interchanges.

The world can be a tiresome place. . .if you can look inside you might find it isn't the stopping point. . .

A story from the pool. . .

There was another day my body lay drenched in weariness. In the mind's eye I reached to a piece of wood - so cool underneath its velvet sheath. Dark wood grained lines moved and flowed until on its tabloid surface I lay spinning deeper into the mist of a mind's spent sleep. Round and round I drifted to a meadow, one sloping its fields to the lips of a wood. Leaving the surface I travest down across the gentle grade. . .the grass stroking my feet until the spread thinned and the soft dust rose from the blades and caressed my ankles.

From the dust, twisted roots raised above, leading on swiftly into the lower valley's of subconscious' deep peace. My feet went on leaving the conscious in its fight to climb upward toward the sun. The trees thickened as did the dust, until out of the arid ground bubbled a creek, dribbling its waters into a shallow bed.

Across the creek I jumped to a rooted ledge and turned to gaze upon the opposite side and there amid the trees were flowers - small petaled blossoms on a fine green carpet - I dropped quietly on the ground resting among the sensuous growth of the shaded bank. As I lay there a shadow settled upon me, and the flowers dulled in the face of it.

Looking around, the centre saw the shadow form. Into the wings of an immense butterfly and i rose on its back over the trees and the stream was covered in the blanket of the forest.

The wings of the giant butterfly glimmered
in the sunlight. All the colors of the cosmos
moved in swirls - binded only by the outline of
the creature's feathered iridescent opaqueness.
    We lit in the plasticized grasses of a higher
meadow from whence lay below the woods through
which I had wandered. This meadow had flowers not
so real in composition - brittle colors pasted on
uniform lines - high gloss green.
    In a web's fiber thought the glossomer insect
rese, leaving me in the upper plateau. Shadows
flecked the hills and the sun then sat in repose.
Bound not by the immobile shell, I returned, in
Circle, to the wooded table again to stroke its
grainy coolness and awakened from the hike refreshed in
spirit – touched by remembrance of a winged creature so
beautiful as to never know visual
reality of my brush.

Strands again. . . cobweb forces of all the energy
        moving in concert within itself –
            intermingling one to - in - of another.

Questions in the pools. . .

Are you there?

No more probably than yesterday,
are you, than now - - -
Maybe less tomorrow.

Where you here?

No more in form did you exist
as i in form - - -
Both illusionary in content.

I saw you. . .

And smelled the smell of beard's
chemistry and touched - - -
the skin - the shell.

I fucked your shell. . .

Loved you on warm cool nights
After cool days in
Thoughts wit-less lare.

The shell was here. . .

Is too the mind, the psychic flow
Present in our private
Daily illusions?
You were there. . .

Touch/taste forms of
A shell's fantasy love. . .
I was there too.

. . . tomorrow I could do a thousand wonders and
if I make no plans there will suffice to be at day fall
no disappointments of the self. . .

   The almighty self. . . the shell of our physical
Inordinate means.
   It is the external shadowing to the vastness of unknown
planes within its tin. The container into
which we lock ourselves like little sardines chocked
in its own fluid.
   What little of the spiritual motion - - that
referred to as the free spirit, which rests in its bed, is damned
to spill its course elsewhere amid the rocks
and pebbles lining the run.
   To exercise the motion - to run the course -
there must be. . .
               (must be: box in the waters loosely so that the motion
might burst the seams and the box (the must of thought)
splinter and dam not the currents within)
               . . .expression of the waters - energy.

   Expression of the currents stirs the floor of the inner bed;
ripples toward the surface and moves onward. It need not
spend its motion on trying to dispel or displace the fragments
of rocks, the illusionary phantoms of solidarity, from their
saucers for the rocks are jaded by their own density and on
their coats, signs of stagnation appear while in the stream that
which is clearest is also deepest and the inner stirrings push
strong in the tides without muddling the spring with silt.

The silt is the waste we confuse with the culture - - the science, the technology, and we misperceive as civilization - progress - marks in our ant hill of mankind.

What life organisms that grow upon the rich, fine silt flourish and reflect in the stream, the health of the land and form en masse the solidarity of the currents.

The spores rooted in the silt would dissolve in the dry winds, into the silt that boast their origin were it not for the cooling, purifying waters washing and feeding their roots.

We are born coming from the seeds spewed from the springs. Our fragile roots grasp the silt, seeking nurturing in a world not so fluid, rather stilted in its awesome concreteness. As our limbs grow we expand upon the self like a tree reaching out to any avenue of life forces - -reaching upward from our woody core - upward to the soothing rains which take away from our touch the dry hollow winds. The rain washes our limbs so that we feel the exposed self washed and livened.

The cracked land upon which we rise and anchor to is moistened and we sparkle, aha! Live! Aware! The sapling, who spins its roots, widely nurturing upon the silt , shoots up glimmering in its physical glory only to wither fast from lack of food for its deepest core.

When the rains wash our shell like the commodities of the shelf washes our 'needs' , the roots remain shallowly fixed in the illusionary life giving, life sustaining silt - the waste - so that we seem blessed in our shell life and 'wants' are reduced.

Unless the roots thrust through the crust and tap the stream, it can not live – - - even the rain must go back to the stream.

Reach out my hand and cup the waters of the sky and the sun evaporates the droplets and the hand is empty.
Let my hand rest gently in the flow, loosely, muscle formless, and the motion is felt by the entire body and the sun can not evaporate the wetness into which my hand is immersed.

Likewise, I open my mind to the torrent of the 'society' and my spirit evaporates and the shell is hollow like the palm, for there is no substance for me. Only from the springs which have washed my spirits when there was no self to be had. . .

From this i live.

I have experienced the many facets of death. Where the events take me in the paths of the living alive i do not comprehend in view of the 'tomorrow' benefits. Nor is the compulsion to understand strong. . .
It just is.

I will always have my anger, my loves, and my aloneness. . .

I will always retain the mutability of shelley's time and regard to it well, the knowledge of the ranging of The Pairs.

I can always hope to be turned and confronted with one that is deeper and out of another consciousness where the experience moves to The Act - the ability to incorporate the cosmic awareness into my life of external concerns. . .

for. . .

the curve of the humanities among us starts its peaking as more individuals touch the inner waters in 'our' universal currents,

then. . .

go we together. . .

in mutual harmony and,

know we together. . .

a river shared.

Made in the USA
Columbia, SC
18 August 2024